# Contents

**Aiming for excellence**

# Foreword by
# The Secretary of State

# Foreword by The Secretary of State

The creation of the Scottish Parliament brings a unique opportunity to shape the future of social work services in Scotland. This White Paper sets out steps which will strike an appropriate balance between protecting vulnerable adults and children whilst enabling them to enjoy ordinary living. Our proposals require legislation which will be for the Scottish Parliament to take forward. We believe that our plans for change will command widespread support and warrant early action by the Parliament.

Social work services tend only to have a high profile when things go wrong. The people who provide these services are rarely given sufficient recognition when they get things right and for the difficult and demanding work that they do. Yet the services are wide ranging and important. They touch most of us, either directly or indirectly. Every day, social work services make a crucial difference to people's lives, whether it is providing the necessary support for people to remain in their own homes and in touch with friends and family, protecting children at risk, or helping offenders to change their offending behaviour. The workforce that provides these services should be recognised as providing a key professional service which requires proper training and regulation. So one part of our proposals is to create a new body – the Scottish Social Services Council – which will register the workforce, put in place a code of conduct and standards to support them, raise professional and training standards, and so raise service standards.

We also believe that services which deal with the most vulnerable people in our society need independent scrutiny. So our second key proposal is to create a Scottish Commission for the Regulation of Care to act as the independent regulator of social work services whoever provides them. The Commission will register organisations that provide care against agreed criteria and make regular independent inspections to see that they are met. It will cover residential care and nursing homes and introduce for the first time regulation of home care services. It will also cover all relevant children's services, and will build on the real improvements brought about by the Children (Scotland) Act 1995, with its crucial emphasis on the child's best interests. The Commission will also regulate some aspects of criminal justice social work services, relating to specialist residential facilities.

More broadly, this White Paper aims to address 3 key questions:

- What kind of social work services do we want?

- How can they be delivered?

- How will we know if they are being delivered effectively?

The Goverment's proposals aim to answer these questions in a way that improves the quality of service provided, offers better safeguards for those being cared for and strengthens professional standards. I am sure that they will command the support of people who use services, their families and carers and staff.

**Rt. Hon. Donald Dewar MP**
Secretary of State for Scotland

# Vision

| # Vision

1.1   People who use the services have clear views of what social work services should be:

- responsive to their individual needs
- reliable
- delivered promptly
- based on best practice and what is known to work.

Some social work services provided by local authorities achieve this, but this is not always the case. This White Paper proposes changes, linked to a number of related themes, which will establish a clear and positive role for social work services in our society – services that deliver what people want.

## Themes

1.2   **Social work services can make a key contribution to social inclusion.** They provide a crucial support to people at times of personal or family crisis. All of us are likely at some point in our lives to have to turn to social work services for support, whether for ourselves or for a family member. Social work services can also help to promote social inclusion, by supporting family and friends in ways that help people to remain active members of the community, and by helping offenders to become better integrated into a purposeful way of life. The Government have recognised the importance of this contribution by making substantial and increased resources available.

1.3   **The social work task is difficult, and needs a competent, confident workforce to deliver it effectively.** Social workers often have to take decisions that are far-reaching, with profound impact on the people they affect. Yet decisions often have to be taken on inadequate or conflicting evidence and in situations of great difficulty. Social workers and social care staff need the support of a strong professional ethos, backed by effective education and training and the guidance of clear codes of conduct and practice.

1.4   **Service standards need to improve to meet the standard of the best.** While some excellent services exist, they are not replicated across the country. We expect more consistent quality to flow from the steps to modernise services and from the development of National Standards. New arrangements for regulation will help to raise standards.

1.5 **Vulnerable people and children need the protection of independent regulation of services.** Regulation is not applied to all services at present and, where it is, there are inconsistencies across the services that are regulated. A national basis for regulation will address both of these shortcomings.

1.6 **Social work services need to work closely with each other and with other agencies in order to deliver services effectively.** The complexity of the social work task, and the need for it to link with other services, requires close and harmonious working within social work, with other statutory agencies, with the voluntary and private sectors, and with other departments within local authorities.

1.7 This is our vision for social work services. To help achieve it, we set out the objectives that social work services should strive to attain.

## Objectives

- To involve people who need care, and those who care for them, in planning services; and tailoring services to their individual care needs with effective measures in place to respond to suggestions.

- To provide effective and efficient social work services, based on the best available evidence of what works, that maximise individual choice and autonomy, demonstrate best value; and allocate resources to needs in a transparent and equitable manner.

- To contribute towards securing an inclusive society that supports individuals, families and children so that they can lead productive and meaningful lives with the help of their communities.

- To ensure that those children for whom the social work services have a legal responsibility receive a standard of care and support that enhances every aspect of their lives.

- To enable adults with social care needs to live as safe, full and normal lives as possible, in their own homes wherever possible.

- To develop and maintain community-based criminal justice services which have the confidence of courts and public.

- To work closely with partner agencies in the NHS, in housing, in education, in criminal justice, and in the voluntary and private sectors.

- To ensure that social care workers are appropriately skilled, trained, qualified and managed to promote the uptake of education and training at all levels.

# Context

# Chapter 2

# Context

2.1 This chapter considers how social work services should be delivered and whether structural change is needed.

## Structural Change

2.2 Social work services are provided or commissioned by local authorities which are responsible for 3 main areas of activity:

- community care
- children's services
- criminal justice social work.

2.3 The effective delivery of all 3 services requires close working relationships with each other, with other departments in the authority and with other agencies. In community care, the key links are with Health Boards and Trusts, housing and education. Children's Services need close links with education, health and criminal justice agencies. Criminal Justice Social Work must work closely with other parts of the social work department, with housing, health, education and employment services, and with the courts, the police and the Prison Service.

2.4 This need for close working has led to the present arrangements being questioned – for example, should community care be provided by Health Boards and Trusts. We have considered these issues carefully, and have reached the following conclusions.

## Community Care

2.5 We consider that the lead responsibility for community care should remain with local authorities. Active involvement of the NHS is crucial, but moving the lead responsibility for community care to the NHS would mean a further period of re-organisation when the need is to concentrate on making the present arrangements work better. The Action Plan, 'Modernising Community Care', published in October 1998, set out priorities for improving close working between local authorities and the NHS. Links with housing are also important, and the present arrangements with social work and housing in the same authorities (and, in a third of councils, in the same department) are working well on most fronts, while developing and improving in other areas. Improved collaborative working is also being promoted through new Housing and Community Care Guidance. Further progress on establishing even closer links between these services would be disrupted if community care were removed from local authority control. **The lead responsibility for community care will therefore remain with local authorities, with other agencies playing a full and important part.**

2.6     The Action Plan emphasised the importance of helping people to stay in their own homes wherever possible, by developing additional and more flexible home care services. It called for better and faster decision making to avoid delays in getting services to people, and targeted resources on authorities with the ability and willingness to take forward this agenda. It placed a new emphasis on joint working, focussing on developing more and better targetted services and new ways to manage and deliver services through local partnerships. It required local authorities and other agencies to have effective local arrangements for joint working in place and operating by March 2000.

2.7     The Action Plan also asked if agencies needed any new powers to help them work more closely together, such as pooled budgets or lead commissioning arrangements. Responses show that some agencies did not see any need for new powers, since the obstacles to close joint working lay more in the areas of working practices, attitudes and culture. These are exactly the areas the Action Plan, and 'Modernising Community Care: the Housing Contribution', seek to address. Other agencies would welcome specific powers to strengthen joint working and the sharing of budgets. We will keep this issue under review as the legislative proposals are developed.

2.8     This White Paper appears just after the publication of the Report of the Royal Commission on Long Term Care of the Elderly. Some recommendations relate to matters such as social security and pensions which are to be reserved to Westminster. Others relate to matters such as social work, health and housing which will be devolved. From 1 July 1999 these will be a matter for the Scottish Parliament and the response to the recommendations will be for the Scottish Executive and Parliament to take forward in the light of the informed debate which the Royal Commission hopes to see, and of the proposals in this White Paper.

## Children's Services

2.9    Children may benefit from a range of social work and associated services. Their need for such services may arise from a range of different circumstances. For example, they may have special needs and disabilities, they may be in need of care and protection or they may need services to address offending behaviour. Children's needs for services may also arise in part from the needs of their parents who may require child care in order that they may work or study. Children who are looked after by local authorities also have educational and health needs. However the complicated issues they face often mean that their health and educational development suffers. To help maximise the child's overall welfare we need to forge the closest links between the children's service, the NHS and education. Improving educational attainment for looked after children is a key part of the Strategic Framework covered in Chapter 4, and children's health is being given particular attention by the NHS following publication of the 'Priorities and Planning Guidance for the NHS in Scotland 1999-2002'. The Public Health White Paper 'Towards a Healthier Scotland'identifies children's health as a priority area.

2.10   How can authorities work to improve the position? One approach is to set up formal machinery to create closer links. Councils may for example, want to convene regular meetings with education and social work to review how well the two services are working together, particularly for children looked after by authorities. We believe that authorities need to take specific steps to ensure that the closest possible working relationships exist for the benefit of children in the authority's care. **Each authority must address this issue and determine what arrangements suit its circumstances best. We will want to be assured, through the Children's Services Plan, that each authority has done so.**

## Criminal Justice Social Work

2.11   The Government consider that there should be maximum use of community based criminal justice disposals and diversion from prosecution consistent with public safety. This requires the courts and the Parole Board to have access to a full range of high quality, robust and effective supervision schemes. The emphasis must be on consistency across the country, collaboration with other parts of the criminal justice system and co-operation with the other services used by offenders. This demands delivery arrangements that focus resources on frontline social work within a clear national framework for policy, standards and enforcement.

2.12   Managing offenders in the community inevitably involves a degree of risk. The Scottish Office has developed a framework for risk assessment in criminal justice social work which is currently being piloted in 16 local authorities. This is an area where effective joint working is essential for public safety. A structured approach to the assessment of risk coupled with the emphasis on research-based effective practice should strengthen supervision in the community and thus enhance public safety.

2.13   The Government issued a consultation paper in September on options for change in the delivery arrangements. Responses are still being considered but no clear consensus has emerged so far. The Government remain committed to finding a solution which improves on the current structure which, with 32 local services, some very small in scale, is not well equipped to deliver a consistent cost effective national service.

## Joint Working

2.14   Although the position is not yet clear for criminal justice social work, we consider that for children's and adult services, Scotland does not need the upheaval of wholesale re-organisation of social work services. While this might remove some boundary problems, others would be created. What we must achieve is more effective close working between services and agencies, a recurring theme of this White Paper. This aim is also relevant to criminal justice, whatever the final decision on delivery arrangements.

2.15   There are interesting initiatives across Scotland of agencies working well together to bring innovative services to people. We will ensure that these are evaluated and best practice promoted. The Government believe there is scope for considerable improvement and that progress must be maintained. The Scottish Parliament will want to keep this under review.

# Assuring Quality

# Assuring Quality

3.1 This chapter considers the oversight necessary to ensure that services deliver what is needed.

## Performance Culture

3.2 This White Paper sets out proposals for strengthening the regulation of social work services and enhancing the professionalism of the workforce. It has ruled out substantial structural change in community care and children's services and made clear that local authorities will continue to be responsible for social work services. Instead, the Government wish to see the maximum effort placed on making the present arrangements work to the best possible effect. To achieve that, the Government want a new relationship with local authorities, with a clear understanding that they are accountable for the considerable resources that are made available to them.

3.3 The Government provided £1050 million for social work services in 1998-1999. This will be increased by £130 million over the next three years. In return, we wish to see movement towards formal review of local authority performance. Some steps have been put in place:

- Some money in the local government financial settlement has been linked to demonstrated performance:

  - for Children's Services, authorities have been invited to submit brief plans on how they intend to commit resources allocated under the Children's Services Development Fund;

  - for Community Care, access to an Action Plan Fund will be dependent on demonstrated progress towards the goals set in the Action Plan;

- For Criminal Justice social work services, the 'Getting Best Results' initiative will help ensure that resources are directed towards practice and projects which can demonstrate effectiveness;

- National Standards already exist for criminal justice social work to help improve efficiency in the delivery of services which are fully funded by Government;

- Authorities must set out for all services how they plan to improve efficiency and effectiveness through submissions under the Best Value initiative.

## Management Information

3.4   The effective management of social work services has been hampered by inadequate management information. Substantial improvement of information systems is needed to enable authorities to see how effective their own services are and compare them with other authorities and the voluntary and private sectors. This will be an integral part of the Best Value process. To that end, we are working jointly with COSLA and the Accounts Commission to review what information is needed and how to collect it, and to develop key performance indicators. These will provide simple measures of performance which are accessible, measure outcomes not inputs and provide a robust basis for comparison between authorities. The National Core Data system for criminal justice social work has been reviewed and streamlined. It will be re-launched in 1999 to inform policy and practice.

## Inspection

3.5   The proposals in this White Paper for an independent Commission to register and inspect all providers of care, including local authorities, will strengthen the emphasis on delivering effective performance locally.

3.6   The national Social Work Services Inspectorate (SWSI) will continue its programme of themed inspections which will focus on strategic issues and be complementary to the local inspection process. SWSI will retain its powers to investigate issues of concern. SWSI will report annually to the Parliament on the delivery of social work services across Scotland.

3.7   The 'Getting Best Results' initiative, involving The Scottish Office, local authorities, the voluntary sector and other key interests, seeks to promote the development of research-based effective practice across all criminal justice social work services. As part of this, we intend to establish an accreditation system for criminal justice social work programmes. The introduction of such a programme to assess quality and to 'kitemark' approved programmes and providers will help achieve greater quality and consistency of services across the country.

## Local Authority Role

3.8    For their part, local authorities will wish to respond to the developing emphasis on performance. It is important that elected members in particular see their role as ensuring that services are delivered in as efficient and effective a manner as possible, and with full recognition of their responsibility for the protection of children and vulnerable adults. Authorities will wish to review their arrangements to ensure that they have clear responsibilities assigned at member level for social work services, including recognised systems for the review of policy and for the effective scrutiny of performance.

3.9    Scrutiny is required at two levels. Firstly, elected members who are responsible for social work must ensure that they have suitable arrangements to inform them of the effectiveness of the performance of the Director of Social Work, or Chief Social Work Officer, and his or her staff. Secondly, members of councils who do not have a direct responsibility for social work have a corporate responsibility for overall council performance, and should therefore be ready to provide a further level of scrutiny of strategic decisions and subsequent performance. Similarly, officials need to be ready to play their part in a more open and more challenging relationship.

## Focus for Change

3.10    In taking all this forward, councillors and officials will need to focus on the key factors for success:

- A strong focus on people
- Effective corporate working within authorities
- Effective partnership working with other agencies
- A rigorous search for cost effectiveness.

3.11    **Strong Focus on People.** The whole thrust of this White Paper has been on the importance of tailoring services to the needs of people rather than fitting people to a limited range of already available services. Authorities need to have ways of monitoring how effectively their services meet people's needs through access to users' and carers' groups at the planning stage, research into people's views and opinions, and an effective and responsive complaints system.

3.12 **Corporate working within local authorities.** The close involvement of other departments within the local authority in the design and delivery of joint services can be crucial to a successful response to the needs of people which often span administrative boundaries. We need to ensure that the different departments within authorities work well together, such as the arrangements suggested for closer working between children's services and education.

3.13 **Partnership working with external agencies.** Equally important is the need to work with different organisations in the statutory, voluntary and private sectors to ensure that people receive effective services which link up well and do not subject them to delays or confusion when their needs cross organisational boundaries.

3.14 **A rigorous search for cost effectiveness.** The Best Value initiative emphasises the importance of delivering services that offer the best balance of cost and quality and closely match people's needs and wishes.

## Annual Reports

3.15 The Government propose that local authorities should produce annual reports covering the effectiveness of the operation of their services. The intention would be for these reports to form part of a rationalisation of the existing planning and reporting systems. These reports would be submitted to the Scottish Administration who in turn would report to the Scottish Parliament. The proposed Commission will also report to the Scottish Administration on the results of its inspections of regulated services. These reports will allow the Scottish Administration and the Parliament to monitor progress and ensure that quality is maintained and developed.

# A Strategic Framework For Children's Services

| # A Strategic Framework For Children's Services

## Introduction

4.1 The needs of children and young people for care and protection cannot be addressed by any one agency on its own. Many of the past failures to nurture and enhance the lives of children who have come into contact with public care agencies stem, at least in part, from an inability to achieve a fully integrated approach to services and professional practice. There are already in place a number of policy initiatives which will make their own impact on better services for children and young people, especially those who may need support to develop their full potential as young adults. Key examples include:

- the **Social Inclusion Strategy,** including particularly the position of children looked after by local authorities and care leavers

- **support for families with very young children** through expansion of family centres

- the **promotion of good parenting** based on an important research report into the provision of parenting programmes and projects across Scotland

- the **Scottish Childcare Strategy** improving the availabilty of quality affordable child care, and pre-school education provision designed to introduce young children early to education and social development

- **new Community Schools** with an emphasis on multi-disciplinary working to assist vulnerable children and families and improve educational attainment.

## Children (Scotland) Act 1995

4.2 The Government are committed to the child-centred policy embodied in the Children (Scotland) Act 1995, its associated regulations and practice guidance. Its 3 key principles are:

- the welfare of the child is paramount
- all statutory intervention with children and families must be justifiable as a better outcome than any other option
- the child should have a voice in decision-making.

4.3    Since its implementation in April 1997 local authorities and other relevant agencies have been developing policies and programmes in line with the Act's provisions. The publication of Children's Services Plans in 1998 marked an important step in making authorities more accountable for those services designed to support children or intervene in their family life. The impact of the Act is being assessed through a structured research programme.

## The Framework

4.4    The Government are committed to working towards the development of a Strategic Framework for Children's Services. This will give a sharper focus to key areas for development, together with measurable targets and outcomes to show progress and allow assessment of performance. It is essential that the Framework should be underpinned by a number of key principles.

## Child Centred Services

4.5    The hallmark of the Children (Scotland) Act 1995 is the promotion and safeguarding of the interests of the child. The introduction of statutory care plans for children looked after by local authorities is designed to ensure that children are treated as individuals, that services match so far as possible individual needs and that authorities fulfil their corporate responsibilities effectively.

## Prevention Through Early Intervention

4.6    There must be a greater focus on early intervention and preventive work with vulnerable children and families. Policies and programmes must be developed further to give priority in terms of management and practitioner time and resource allocation to tackling this essential area.

## Improvements in Service Quality

4.7    There must be a greater emphasis on quality community placements, including expansion of foster care. At the same time improvements in residential care standards through the use of smaller units and better qualified staff is of equal importance. These quality developments must go forward as complementary not alternative strategies.

## Multi-Agency Working

4.8　The needs of the whole child should be addressed. This requires effective working together by health, education, social work and other agencies. There is scope for more integrated approaches to early intervention, child protection and supporting children looked after by local authorities. Children's Services Plans should reflect fully co-ordinated analysis and planning across all relevant sectors.

## Securing Better Outcomes

4.9　The overall objective must be to identify and secure focused outcomes for Children's Services in terms of:

- the social and emotional development of the individual child

- educational attainment

- avoidance of anti-social or criminal behaviour.

## Children's Services Development Fund

4.10　Detailed work to expand the principles and develop performance indicators will continue so that the Strategic Framework for Children's Services can be taken forward under the new Parliament. However the Government have already indicated very clearly their commitment to starting that process now. In November 1998 the Government Response to the Kent Report 'Children's Safeguards Review' included the establishment of a Children's Services Development Fund with an extra £37 m over the next 3 years. The Fund is intended to lever change in 3 key areas for development:

- expansion of foster care services

- greater advocacy services for children looked after by local authorities

- expansion of family centres for more preventive work with families with very young children.

4.11　In these critical areas a fresh start can be made, building on good practice and the extra resources from the Development Fund. We believe that a qualitative difference can be made now to the lives of the most vulnerable children in our society if we secure the improvements intended from this extra investment over the 3 years.

## Child Protection – Improved Safeguards

4.12 Child protection work continues to make heavy demands on local authorities and other agencies. Considerable resources are deployed by agencies to protect children from abuse or the risk of abuse and to help those who have been victims. Despite these efforts many children continue to suffer harm and neglect.

4.13 The Children (Scotland) Act 1995 introduced new and improved child protection measures and these were complemented by the publication in November 1998 of revised inter-agency child protection guidance 'Protecting Children – A Shared Responsibility'. The guidance indicated that many children at risk of harm live in families in which social exclusion, domestic violence, mental illness or misuse of drugs or alcohol are significant factors. Good health care, education and family support are essential services to safeguard and promote children's welfare. They can also strengthen the capacity of families under stress to meet the needs of their children before problems escalate to abuse or neglect.

4.14 Preventive strategies are critically important when children are looked after and cared for away from the family home. As part of such strategies, local authorities and other care providers need to have in place rigorous staff selection procedures. Those engaging staff (or volunteers) must be satisfied that recruits are qualified and/or have relevant experience for the particular post. They must also ensure that they do not allow unsuitable persons to obtain access to children in their charge.

## Consultancy Index

4.15 The Government are committed to doing more to improve safeguards for children at risk by developing a fully comprehensive approach to information held about those unsuitable to work with children and young people. As part of that strategy the Secretary of State announced on 5 November 1998 his intention to introduce a statutory Consultancy Index for Scotland. This formed part of the Government Response to the Kent Report 'Children's Safeguards Review.'

4.16    At present the main source of information on individuals deemed unsuitable to work with children and young people is the criminal record information held by the Scottish Criminal Record Office. This can be supplemented by details of teachers who may have been removed from the Register of the General Teaching Council for Scotland or, in the case of teachers in England and Wales, banned by the Secretary of State for Education and Employment on grounds of misconduct. Comparable information will be held in due course by the new Scottish Commission for Regulation of Care. However, there may also be less formal sources of information about unsuitable individuals beyond that recorded for criminal conviction purposes. The Government believe it is right to provide a statutory framework with appropriate legal safeguards to establish a database for the holding and dissemination of such information.

4.17    The Consultancy Index will contain information provided by employers about staff (including volunteers) whom they consider unsuitable to work with children by reason of misconduct which harmed a child or placed a child at risk. Employers in child care organisations would be required to supply the Index with information about such individuals. Other organisations would be able to do so.

4.18    Before employing someone in a child care position, employers would be required to check the name of the prospective employee (or volunteer) against the information held in the Index. Where it is found that the prospective employee's (or volunteer's) name is held on the Index the employer would be prohibited from employing the individual in a child care position. There will be a formal appeals mechanism under which the individual may contest the inclusion of his or her name on the Index.

4.19    The Government recognise that there are important legal and civil liberties issues connected with the storage and dissemination of non-conviction information. Nonetheless reservations on these matters are outweighed by the need to introduce measures which go as far as possible to protect children from those who may have ulterior motives for wishing to work with them. This measure forms part of a longer term aim to bring together information from a number of sources so that employers and others who take on staff or volunteers to work with children have a single access point for advice about a person's suitability or otherwise for such a post.

4.20    The Government propose that, as soon as is practicable, the Index should be expanded to include people who have been found unsuitable to work with vulnerable adults. This will be done when experience has been gained of operating the Index for children.

# Regulations of Care Services

| # Regulation of Care Services

5.1 There are 42,000 vulnerable people living in residential care homes, children's homes and nursing homes in Scotland. There are many others, often cared for by relatives, some socially isolated, who receive social care in their own homes. Effective regulation of those services, and of the staff who provide them, is essential if the people themselves and their families are to have confidence that the care they receive will be competent and reliable. The current Act controlling the regulation of nursing homes dates from 1938 and that for residential care homes from 1968. There is widespread support for updating this legislation and for the introduction of regulation of care given to people in their own homes which at present has no formal system of regulation.

5.2 The current legislation governing the regulation of day care for children, the Children Act 1989, requires those who provide day care and childminding services for children under 8 to register with the local authority; and the local authority is required to inspect those services at least once a year. Although this is a relatively new regulatory regime it too is in need of modernisation, particularly in view of the expansion in services which is taking place.

5.3 The Government therefore propose that the regulation of these services should be reformed to provide better safeguards for vulnerable adults and for children. Our plans are based on the principles of good regulation set out by the Better Regulation Taskforce:

 - Transparency
 - Accountability
 - Targeting
 - Consistency
 - Proportionality.

## Problems with the Current System

5.4 As indicated above, the existing arrangements for regulating care services were developed in piecemeal fashion. Residential care homes in the voluntary and private sectors are regulated by local authorities and nursing homes are regulated by Health Boards. Residential care homes run by councils are not subject to the same regulation, and nor is support to people at home, irrespective of who provides it. Day care services for children under 8 are also regulated by local authorities.

5.5    This leads to a number of problems:

**Lack of Independence** – Local authorities are responsible for regulating residential care homes from which they purchase services and which are in competition with the council's own homes. Councils are responsible for purchasing, providing and regulating residential care. There is therefore a potential conflict of interest.

**Lack of Consistency** – There are 32 local authorities and 15 Health Boards responsible for regulating care homes. Standards inevitably vary across Scotland, creating uncertainty for both the people who use services, and those that provide them. Smaller councils may not be able to employ the range of specialist staff required.

**Lack of Integration** – The separate regulatory regime for nursing homes makes it difficult for home owners to provide both nursing home and residential care home services from the one establishment.

Of course the present system also has a number of strengths, such as the provision of advice and guidance to providers. These should be safeguarded in the new system.

## Proposals

5.6    Our proposals to modernise the system of regulation will:

– **Create** a Scottish Commission for the Regulation of Care (SCRC) which will be responsible for the regulation of social work services

– **Introduce** statutory regulation for care at home and extend the regulation of day care

– **Improve** the way in which registration and inspection are carried out.

These proposals build on the Report of the Working Group on Residential Care Home Registration Procedures, published in 1996, which had a widely drawn representative membership. They will require legislative action which will be for the Scottish Parliament to take forward.

## Scottish Commission for the Regulation of Care

5.7 To ensure the necessary independent structure for registration, we will establish a Scottish Commission for the Regulation of Care (SCRC). It will over time be responsible for registration, inspection and enforcement of standards, for the following care services:

- residential care homes for adults in the private, voluntary and local authority sectors

- nursing homes

- specialist residential accommodation for offenders

- care at home

- day care for adults

- some forms of supported accommodation

- adoption

- fostering

- day-care for children

- children's residential care homes

- secure accommodation for children.

Regulation of these services will be achieved by registering service providers who qualify against agreed criteria. The present responsibility of local authorities for registration and inspection for social care, and of Health Boards for nursing homes, will cease.

5.8 The Commission will be an independent statutory body with the power to act in its own right, but will be accountable to the Scottish Administration and through that to the Scottish Parliament. Scottish Ministers will have powers of direction and guidance over the Commission and will appoint its Chair and a management board, including representatives from local authorities and Health Boards, and from user and provider organisations. There will be recourse to the Parliamentary Commissioner for Administration (or successor arrangements) for complaints against the Commission's exercise of its duties, as well as the right to appeal against de-registration or refusal of registration to an Appeals Tribunal (see paragraph 5.42).

5.9 The Commission will have its own team of inspectors and will decide how they should be deployed to achieve good geographical coverage. The Inspectorate team will consist of people with skills and qualifications from social work and other relevant disciplines, including health.

## Standards

5.10 At present different authorities require registered organisations to meet different standards because there is no national consensus on standards. The Government propose to move quickly to establish a National Care Standards Committee with the task of developing, through a process of consultation, a series of National Standards for the services regulated by the Commission. When the Commission is established following the necessary legislation, it will take on the responsibility for consulting on National Standards and recommending changes to the Scottish Administration.

# Scope of Regulation

## Residential Care Homes and Nursing Homes

5.11 Regulation will apply, as now, to residential care homes and nursing homes, although there will be improvements to the way this operates. In addition, all residential care homes owned by local authorities themselves will be required to register, and will be subject to inspection and enforcement procedures in the same way as voluntary and private care homes.

5.12 Bringing together nursing homes and residential care homes under one regulatory authority will enable providers to offer a more flexible service. Homes will be capable of being registered for either category or for both, for all or part of their places. This will enable them to bring in extra support to residents who become more frail, without the difficulties associated with dealing with two different systems of registration and inspection, and avoid the trauma of a move to a different home for the resident.

5.13 Health Boards will cease to have responsibility for the regulation of nursing homes with the creation of the Commission. They will wish to liaise closely with the Commission on issues of common interest, including their capacity to provide supporting health services to residential care homes or nursing homes, particularly when new homes are seeking to be registered.

5.14 The terms of registration should be flexible enough to enable homes to adjust staffing and other facilities rapidly when the number of residents in the home changes.

## Specialist Residential Accommodation for Offenders

5.15    The Government recognise that some offenders require to be accommodated in specialist residential facilities for a period of time to ensure the necessary levels of supervision of their behaviour. Specialised facilities such as residential hostels and dispersed accommodation which includes a 'care' element will be subject to regulation by the Commission. National Standards for this care element will be developed in due course, as set out in paragraph 5.10 above.

## Care at Home

5.16    Support provided to people in their own homes is an essential part of good community care. The Action Plan, 'Modernising Community Care', made clear that the Government wanted to see more care provided at home. Care at home is what most people want, and it is a central means of sustaining independence and promoting social inclusion. Regulation of this key service will provide reassurance to vulnerable users while maintaining the principles of choice and independence.

5.17    The regulation scheme will be based on registering the organisations providing personal social care to people living in their own homes rather than the individual employees of the organisations. Self-employed individuals offering these services will not be registered under the scheme, although the scheme may be extended in the future to cover them. The scheme will not cover organisations which provide services of a purely non-care nature, for example cleaning agencies, although it may be extended to these in the future.

5.18    The Comissions will register organisations if they demonstrate that they meet the required criteria and standards. These will be developed by the National Care Standards Committee in consultation with interested parties, and are likely to cover areas such as:

- fitness of owner and manager

- personnel issues, (including recruitment and vetting procedures, personnel records, policies on training, health and safety, equal opportunities etc)

- information to users (e.g. on charges, service withdrawals, how to complain etc)

- quality procedures (e.g. including complaints procedures, systems for monitoring users' satisfaction, supervision of care staff etc)

- operational policies (e.g. administration of medicines, confidentiality, health and safety, promotion of choice, access to users' homes etc)

- financial viability and insurance.

## Day Care for Adults

5.19 Day care is an important part of community services, giving support and the opportunity for meaningful activities. It is particularly valuable to people with learning disabilities but other community care client groups also benefit. Not all day care is at present subject to formal regulation and users would benefit from the oversight of regulation. The Government propose that once the Commission is established and has taken on the new task of regulating care at home, it should then develop the registration and inspection of day care providers.

## Supported Accommodation

5.20 Supported accommodation is housing provided with additional services to help the residents to live as independently as possible. These services are normally limited to support, for example warden schemes in sheltered housing developments, but they can extend to include care services provided at home. In the absence of regulation of care provided at home, some supported housing projects have been registered as residential care homes. This is only appropriate where the care services are of a substantial or intensive nature. With the introduction of regulation of care provided at home, the care services brought into supported accommodation projects will themselves be regulated, and in many cases this will be more appropriate than registering the project as a residential care home. This will also provide an opportunity for the Commission to reconsider existing projects which are registered as residential care homes to see if this is still appropriate. Receiving regulated care services at home would not affect people's status as tenants.

5.21 The low level support which enables many vulnerable people to live independently within the community is presently funded from a variety of sources and relies on an uncertain funding base. The Government therefore published on 10 December 1998 a consultation paper 'Supporting People: A New Policy and Funding Framework for Support Services'. This proposes that, in the long-term, current expenditure on support services would be transferred into a single budget – Supporting People – to be corporately administered by the housing and social work services arms of the local authority. The consultation period ended on 5th February 1999 and responses are currently being analysed.

## Adoption

5.22    Local authority provision of adoption services is governed by primary and subordinate legislation. However the standards of the services are not subject at present to routine independant scrutiny. This is no longer acceptable. The Government propose therefore that local authority adoption services should be within the scope of the Commission.

5.23    Voluntary agencies providing adoption services in Scotland are subject to independent oversight through primary and subordinate legislation. They must be approved by the Secretary of State. This is normally discharged through periodic inspection by the Social Work Services Inspectorate with recommendations as to the continued registration and approval of individual agencies. In the interests of ensuring consistency of approach across the public and voluntary sectors it is proposed that the direct role of the Secretary of State should be discontinued and his responsibilities discharged in future by the Commission.

## Fostering

5.24    There are at present no statutory requirements governing the inspection and registration of fostering services, either with local authorities or voluntary or private sector agencies. Local authorities entering into arrangements with voluntary agencies must be satisfied that appropriate standards are being met. However the trend towards placements for older children with more challenging behaviour and needs has increased the demands and expectations on these services. The case for improving quality and protection by bringing fostering services within the inspection and registration process is therefore strong.

5.25    It is proposed that the local authority foster placement service should be registered and inspected. This will include inspecting the approval and support of foster carers and the general operation of the Fostering Panel.

5.26    At present local authorities may make arrangements with a voluntary sector fostering agency if they are satisfied that it can discharge fostering services on the authority's behalf. The responsibility for assessing the capacity of such organisations will pass to the Commission who will inspect and register all voluntary agencies.

5.27    There have been suggestions from time to time that fostering services could be provided on a commercial basis. **The Government invite views on the case for allowing local authorities to enter into arrangements with private fostering agencies, and whether such agencies should be subject to inspection and registration by the new body.**

## Private Fostering

5.28 Private fostering is quite separate to all other types of fostering. It is a private arrangement entered into between a parent and another person not related to the child where it is proposed that the child is cared for by the other person for a period of more than 28 days. There are probably few such arrangements in Scotland, but the fact that a child can be living away from home for such a period of time could be a matter for concern.

5.29 Both parent and carer are required to notify the local authority in advance of the arrangement, and on receiving such notification the authority visits the carer's place of residence to satisfy itself that the welfare of the child will be adequately safeguarded. In view of the vulnerability of children in such arrangements the Government propose that the local authority's duties in this regard will be inspected as part of the Commission's oversight of the provision of fostering services.

## Day Care for Children

5.30 The Government are investing substantial sums through the Scottish Childcare Strategy in improving and extending the provision of day care services for children. At present most formal day care provided for children under the age of 8 is subject to registration under the Children Act 1989. Day care services provided by local authorities are inspected by their own inspection units. Day care provided from other sources is subject to inspection by local authorities as a condition of registration. Childminders are inspected and registered by local authorities.

5.31 There is a wide range of day care facilities across the public, private and voluntary sectors. Improving the quality of care for all children, including their safety, the standards of facilities and the wider links with social, educational and economic development for children and families are all key components in the Government's Scottish Childcare Strategy. Given the variety and diversity of facilities providing day care, it is all the more important to ensure that the highest standards possible are achieved in the interests of the children concerned and the well being of their families.

5.32 The Government propose therefore that all day care services will in future be subject to registration and inspection by the Commission. This will include all local authority day care provision, private and voluntary sector facilities and childminders. There may be a case for extending the coverage of day care regulation beyond that provided for in the 1989 Act, for example in relation to the age range of children whose care is regulated. Issues of this kind are being examined in the context of the consultation paper on the regulation of early education and childcare being published alongside this White Paper.

5.33 Where day care and pre-school education are provided in the same facilities, responsibility for registration and inspection of the education components will remain with Her Majesty's Inspectorate of Schools.

## Children's Residential Care Homes

5.34 All residential children's establishments providing services for the purposes of the Children (Scotland) Act 1995 are currently required to be registered if they are managed by voluntary or private organisations. Residential services provided by local authorities themselves are not regulated in this way. The Government consider the present position to be inequitable.

5.35 It is proposed therefore that all such residential establishments for children will in future be registered and inspected through the Commission, whether they operate in the local authority, voluntary or private sectors. Registration and inspection will also extend to educational establishments required to register under social work provisions, and those choosing to do so voluntarily.

## Secure Accommodation for Children

5.36 Some of the most damaged and vulnerable children and young people in our society may be placed in secure accommodation units. At present all secure accommodation facilities are subject to approval by the Secretary of State. Those operated by local authorities are subject to authorities' own internal inspection procedures. All units provided by independent organisations are registered and approved directly by the Secretary of State on the basis of SWSI inspection reports.

5.37 As part of the drive towards ensuring a comprehensive and consistent approach to these important facilities the Government propose that all registration responsibilities, including those currently exercised by the Secretary of State, should transfer to the Commission. However, statutory approval of secure units will be retained by Ministers of the Scottish Parliament.

## Boarding Schools

5.38 Proprietors of boarding schools have a duty to promote the care and welfare of children residing in their accommodation. HM Inspectors of Schools currently undertake inspections of boarding schools' care and welfare provision under section 66 of the Education (Scotland) Act 1980. The Government have no plans at present to regulate these schools' care and welfare provision under the Commission, but will keep the matter under review.

## Other Services

5.39   Field social work will not be subject to regulation. However the legislation we propose to introduce will be sufficiently flexible to allow the scheme of regulation to be extended if there is a need to do so.

## Inspection

5.40   Once a provider organisation is registered, it will be subject to annual review by the Commission and may also be inspected at any time. The inspection may involve a variety of methods, such as scrutiny of records, interviews with staff and sample interviews with users, in order to check whether registration standards continue to be met.

## Enforcement

5.41   All services that are registered will be subject to appropriate enforcement action. This will include powers to impose conditions, to report serious cases to the Procurator Fiscal and where necessary to de-register, including emergency de-registration. The aim will be to ensure greater consistency in enforcement practice.

5.42   Formal appeals against the Commission's decisions will be made, as now, to an Appeals Tribunal convened for the purpose from a standing panel of experts, chaired by a Sheriff. Measures will be introduced, in line with the recommendations of the 1996 report of the Working Group, to speed up the progress of cases to make it simpler and less expensive.

## Resources

5.43   Resources reflecting the present cost of regulation will transfer from local authorities and Health Boards to the Commission. There will be provision for central funding of the Commission, but the Government's aim is for the cost of regulation to be met by fees paid by regulated providers.

# Regulation of the Workforce

# Regulation of the Workforce

6.1   More than 100,000 people work in social care settings in Scotland. Half of them are employed in local authorities, while the remainder work in private and voluntary agencies. People using social work services have a right to expect high quality services delivered by a competent workforce committed to continuous improvement. Though this is usually the case, sadly it is not always so. There have been well-documented examples of the abuse of adults and children who use the services. This reflects adversely on the competence and integrity of a workforce whose members are in large part committed and dedicated.

6.2   The Government recently consulted on workforce regulation and education (Modernising Social Work Services, a Consultation Paper on Workforce Regulation and Education, 1998). Almost 150 responses have been received from a wide range of stakeholders. The Government are grateful for many thoughtful and helpful comments received. They have been taken into account in the framing this White Paper and will contribute to the implementation of the proposals on workforce regulation and education. There were over 50 suggestions for the name of the new regulatory body. The Government have decided that the body shall be called the Scottish Social Services Council.

## Scottish Social Services Council

6.3   The Government propose to create a Scottish Social Services Council (SSSC) which will register staff in certain key groups as a pre-condition before they can be employed or can continue in employment. The Government's prime concern in regulating staff in the social work services is to strengthen and support the professionalism of the workforce, raise service standards, and thus protect and benefit the people who use these services.

6.4   It will be the Council's job to improve the quality of services by raising standards in the workforce. It will maintain a register of staff and make sure that more staff get the education and training and qualifications they need for the jobs they do. The Government mean to set up similar bodies across the UK and the Council in Scotland will wish to work closely with these counterparts.

6.5 The Council will be an independent statutory body subject to regulation by the Scottish Parliament. Given its key functions of regulating the workforce and developing its training and education, the Council needs to be responsive to a number of interests. These include the workforce, people who use its services, their carers, the public, professional associations, employers, education providers and the Government. Members of the Council will therefore be appointed to reflect these interests.

## The Key Functions of the new Body

6.6 The Government propose that the Council should have powers to:

- register, discipline (by fine or suspension) or impose conditions (eg by requirements to re-train) or de-register individual members

- recognise courses leading to certain qualifications

- require employers to demonstrate that they meet requirements for employment, supervision and training of specified staff

- co-operate with related bodies within the UK and promote international learning within social services.

## Key activities will be to:

- maintain registers of specified groups of staff

- regulate professional and vocational education

- publish codes of conduct and practice for all staff.

## Maintaining Registers of Staff

6.7 Most professional regulatory bodies use some form of register to set and maintain standards for entering and staying in the workforce. The Government believe that registration of individuals has an important part to play in strengthening public confidence. We also believe that the Council should use its registration powers to drive up levels of education, training and qualifications. The primary role of the Council will therefore be to register the workforce having regard to education and training achievements.

6.8     The social care workforce is large, diverse and in large part unqualified, and the overall approach to registration will have to reflect this. The Government have consulted a wide range of interests in Scotland on whether the register should seek to cover the whole workforce or whether it should start with a smaller group, building a clear link between qualifications, registration and employment.

6.9     Although there is support for moving immediately to register the whole workforce, the Government believe that such an approach would undermine the key aim of registration which is to raise standards. We therefore propose to identify priority groups, such as residential child care staff, and require them to complete approved courses of training as a pre-condition for registration. A timetable will be set by regulation within which staff would be required to complete their training requirements. At the end of the timetable period, it would no longer be possible to work in the priority area without being registered, and registration would be dependent on having completed the required training. Thus a clear link would be established between registration, possession of a defined qualification, and employment. In relation to child care, the Government have launched a residential child care training initiative with a view to introducing an accessible and flexible national training resource in the course of the next financial year.

6.10    For professionally qualified social workers, the steps to registration would be more direct, as they would be eligible for registration on the basis of their existing qualification plus a period of approved practical experience. As most would meet both these requirements, they would move immediately to registration.

6.11    The groups of staff who would be required to register in the first wave following the creation of the Council would be:

- All people occupying a designated social worker post in any sector
- All people with a professional social work qualification (the Diploma in Social work or its equivalent) working in, or wishing to work in a social work field
- All Heads of residential care homes
- All staff in residential child care.

Other groups of staff will be phased in over time as their training requirements are set and achieved. On present plans, it is not intended that all groups will necessarily be registered. Other systems will provide protection in respect of groups not included – such as employer checks required by the registration of employing organisations and the Consultancy Index described in Chapter 4 which will include the names of people considered unsuitable to work with children. The Council will work closely with the Consultancy Index.

6.12    The Council will have the power to de-register individuals for breach of the codes of conduct or practice. There will be formal mechanisms for de-registration which may provide for hearings to determine the facts and adjudicate the matter. This will operate in a way that gives proper weight to the interests of the service-users concerned. There will also be powers for urgent suspension in serious cases, prior to the full hearing of the issues. There will be a right of appeal against de-registration. Less serious cases might require the imposition of conditions, such as a requirement to undertake specified training.

## Job Reservation and Protection of Title

6.13    In some professions or occupational groups, the law restricts employment to particular groups of people. Within social care there are jobs which carry a statutory restriction on employment. For example, there is a statutory requirement that Mental Health Officers and Chief Social Work Officers have particular qualifications. This is because the functions that they undertake are complex or specialised. The Government believe that this is necessary for some jobs and proposes that the proposed regulation should provide powers to introduce job reservation or the protection of title where it concludes that these offer useful safeguards.

## Regulating Professional and Vocational Education

6.14    Currently, the Central Council for Education and Training in Social Work (CCETSW) has responsibility for promoting, developing and regulating education and training at all levels and awarding qualifications in social work. The Government intend that following legislation, CCETSW will be wound up and its essential functions transferred. Promotion of education of social care and social work staff is the shared responsibility of CCETSW, employers, education providers and The Scottish Office. Government policy is to introduce National Training Organisations (NTOs) which will place the responsibility on employers to identify the education, training and skills needs of their businesses and their employees. The Government recently approved the creation of the Training Organisation for the Personal Social Services (TOPSS) to develop and promote training at all levels. This NTO has UK-wide functions and is currently led by CCETSW.

6.15    Following the wind up of CCETSW, the NTO functions would be undertaken by the Council. This will ensure productive links between the NTO functions, particularly training needs and the development of occupational standards, and the regulatory functions in relation to codes of practice and qualifications in social work. The Council will work closely with other relevant NTOs, including those for early years, the health service, the voluntary sector, local government and community justice.

6.16 In Scotland, the Scottish Qualifications Authority (SQA) awards Scottish Vocational Qualifications (SVQs) in social work. The Government's proposal to create a Council to regulate the workforce will give a new focus for the development of social work education. The Council will have a very important role in developing and regulating vocational education in social work and an advisory role towards the SQA. Giving the Scottish Social Services Council this role will align it with similar bodies, such as the General Teaching Council, which act as a key stepping-stone from full-time education to employment.

## Publishing Codes of Conduct and Practice

6.17 The Government recognise that the majority of staff carry out their work well and with humanity often in situations of great difficulty. The Government believe that staff will be helped in their work if they are guided by a set of enforceable codes of conduct and practice. Such codes will enable users and the public to know what standards they can expect of staff. They will also guide all staff and their employers in a common understanding of conduct and practice requirements. These should include the personal responsibility of individuals for their continuing education and the development and maintenance of their own practice standards. The Government propose that the Council should have the necessary powers to set standards and that drawing up the codes will be an important part of their task.

6.18 Adherence to these codes of conduct and practice will be a condition of employment enforced by service regulation. The Government have no wish to usurp or duplicate the responsibilities of employers. The new arrangements will need to be aligned with employer responsibilities.

6.19 Conduct or practice may sometimes fall short of the accepted standards. Where this is not so serious as to warrant de-registering or the imposition of conditions, the Government see this as the responsibility of employers. The Council will, therefore, draw up complementary codes of practice for employers on recruitment, management and supervision, disciplinary mechanisms, complaints, staff education and training and development. Employers will be expected to develop systems of annual appraisal of their staff to maintain competence in accordance with these codes.

6.20 The Scottish Office is currently funding a consortium of local authorities, led by Perth and Kinross, to develop a code of practice to govern recruitment for staff working with children. We expect the results of this work to pave the way for further work by the Council. The code of practice for employers will be enforced even-handedly in the services regulated by the Commission through National Standards (described in the previous chapter). Where necessary the code will be enforced in the statutory sector using the powers of direction and guidance which will devolve to the Ministers of the Scottish Parliament.

## Resources

6.21 The cost of regulating the workforce will be met from fees paid by registrants on a yearly basis. There will be a sliding scale for the different categories on the register, taking account of differential pay scales. The Government currently fund the regulation of education and training through its funding of CCETSW and these funds will be transferred to the Council.

6.22 The Government believe that these proposals represent a major step towards supporting and enhancing the professionalism of social work staff. This will benefit not only the workforce, but all those who use social work services.

# Summary and Conclusion

| # Summary and Conclusion

## Vision

7.1 This White Paper sets out the Government's proposals for achieving a modern and dependable social work service. Such a service should be responsive to individual needs, reliable and delivered promptly. The task is a difficult one, and needs a competent, confident workforce to deliver it effectively. Vulnerable adults and children need the protection of independent regulation of the services they receive. These proposals aim to create such a service.

## Partnership

7.2 The Government do not wish to waste energy on structural reorganisation; the lead responsibility for children's and adult social services will remain with local authorities. What is needed is more effective joint working between services and agencies. While there are interesting examples of innovative practice and partnership working, we believe there is scope for considerable improvement and that progress must be maintained.

## Achieving Quality

7.3 The Comprehensive Spending Review identified significant additional resources for social work services. These must be well deployed. We wish to see local authorities taking a positive and pro-active approach with councillors and officials working to ensure that services are delivered in as flexible, efficient and effective a way as possible, with full recognition of their responsibility for the protection of children and vulnerable adults. The key factors for success are:

- a strong focus on people
- effective corporate working within authorities
- effective partnership working with other agencies
- a rigorous search for cost effectiveness.

7.4 The Government are determined to improve the quality of children's services, building on the child-centred approach embodied in the Children (Scotland) Act 1995. A Strategic Framework for Children's Services aims to secure clear outcomes in terms of:

- the social and emotional development of the individual child
- educational attainment
- avoidance of anti-social or criminal behaviour.

7.5 The Government believe that staff will be helped in their difficult and demanding work if they are supported by a professional body to set and maintain standards, regulate professional and vocational education and publish codes of conduct and practice. Our proposals will:

- create an independent statutory body, the Scottish Social Services Council (SSSC)
- improve the quality of services by raising standards in the workforce
- rationalise education and training.

## Improving Protection

7.6 Existing child protection measures will be strengthened by a statutory Consultancy Index holding information provided by employers about staff whom they consider unsuitable to work with children and young people. In due course, the Index should be expanded to include people found unsuitable to work with vulnerable adults. Regulation of the workforce will also offer additional safeguards for vulnerable people.

7.7 The Government's proposals will modernise the system of service regulation and provide a service which is independent and consistent, and which integrates the regulation of residential care homes and nursing homes. They will:

- create a new independent regulatory body, the Scottish Commission for the Regulation of Care (SCRC)
- introduce statutory regulation for care provided at home, and expand the regulation of day care
- improve the way in which registration and inspection are carried out.

Registered organisations will be subject to annual reviews and may be inspected at any time. Standards will be enforced by the imposition of conditions and when necessary de-registration. The existing appeals system will be improved to speed up progress of appeals.

## Conclusion

7.8 Social work services play a key role in working with some of the most vulnerable members of society. They can provide a bridge out of dependence, isolation and exclusion. If enacted by the Scottish Parliament, the proposals in this White Paper offer people who use social work services the assurance of independent regulation of these services and of key staff who provide them. They offer children more clearly focused services for those that need them and enhanced protection for those in care. They offer the workforce clarity about the future of the service and a statutory professional body to support them and raise professional and training standards. These proposals will strengthen public confidence, creating modern social work services on which we can all rely.

Printed in the UK for The Stationery Office Ltd
on behalf of the Controller of Her Majesty's Stationery Office
Dd 293578 C80 3/99 3312